25 Projects
for Global Explorers

ALA Editions purchases fund advocacy, awareness, and accreditation programs for library professionals worldwide.

25 Projects for Global Explorers

CHRISTINE M. KIRKER

ALA Editions
CHICAGO | 2019

Christine M. Kirker is a library associate with the Carroll County (Maryland) Public Library. Since joining the library staff in 2005, Christine has developed and presented many programs for adults and children of all ages, including Science and Art Explorers programs. Christine is the author of *25 Projects for Art Explorers* (ALA Editions, 2018). Christine, with Kathy MacMillan, has co-authored five books published with ALA Editions: *Storytime Magic* (2009), *Kindergarten Magic* (2011), *Multicultural Storytime Magic* (2012), *Baby Storytime Magic* (2014), and *More Storytime Magic* (2016).

ISBN: 978-0-8389-1885-2 (paper)

Library of Congress Cataloging in Publication Control Number: 2019007202

Book cover by Kimberly Thornton. Composition by Alejandra Diaz in the Cardea and the Vista Slab typefaces.

♾ This paper meets the requirements of ANSI/NISO Z39.48-1992 (Permanence of Paper).

Printed in the United States of America
23 22 21 20 19 5 4 3 2 1

FOR CHRIS

Thanks for listening to my ideas and exploring the world with me.

contents

PART II: EXPLORING OTHER COUNTRIES

introduction

With the emphasis to begin incorporating STEM activities (science, technology, engineering, and mathematics) to children at earlier ages, often neglected is the idea of exploring subjects outside the sciences. Schools must meet curriculum goals with standardized testing beginning at earlier ages, leaving little time for creativity and imagination. *25 Projects for Global Explorers* will spark children's interest in the history, geography, events, and landmarks around the world, and encourage creativity, collaboration, and critical thinking. Children are introduced to a variety of places that make our world unique and special. Each topic is presented through the lens of a representative picture book. Children will learn about what makes the topic special and complete a hands-on project. *Global Explorers* will reinforce learning, encourage experimentation, and build an appreciation for the world. *Global Explorers* will also encourage children to take a break from our increasingly virtual screen-filled world and explore the real world around them.

PART I

Exploring the United States of America

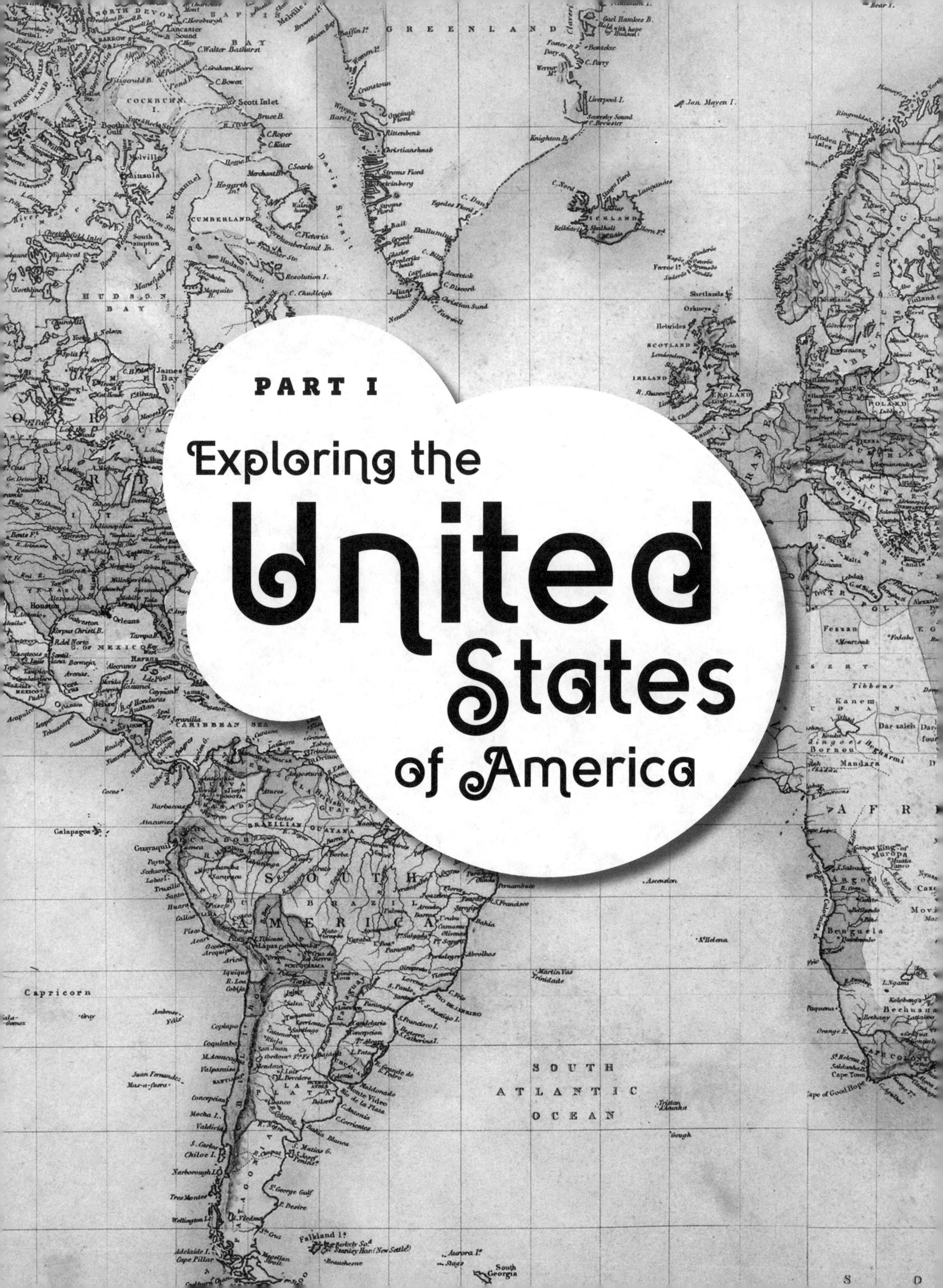

1

Iditarod Trail Sled Dog Race

ALASKA

If You Were a Kid at the Iditarod
Josh Gregory. New York, NY: Scholastic Inc, 2018.

A young boy visits his cousins in Alaska during the Iditarod race. While the fictional story tells of the family following his cousin's race, facts about the Iditarod race and dogs are included on each page. The story is engaging for children, and the added information makes learning the details of the race interesting for all.

Programming Tip

The Iditarod Trail Sled Dog Race is an annual event each March. You can use a GPS tracker to follow the race on your computer. Share this event while learning about sled dog teams and the geography of the trail. You can get a GPS Tracker subscription at http://iditarod.com/gps/.

ABOUT THE IDITAROD

The Iditarod Trail Sled Dog Race is an annual long-distance race held in early March. The trail runs from Anchorage to Nome and is nearly 1,000 miles long. Each sled dog team consists of 16 dogs and a musher to drive the dogs. Although many believe the Iditarod Race was originally established to commemorate the delivery of a diphtheria antitoxin to Nome in 1925, it was actually established in 1973 to preserve the culture of the sled dogs and their place in Alaskan history. The Iditarod trail was the original route used by Native Alaskans to travel to other villages and provided a way to supply miners at settlements with mail and other necessities. The Serum Run race commemorates the delivery of the diphtheria antitoxin and only covers part of the original Iditarod Trail. The Iditarod Trail is a Congressionally designated National Historic Trail in Alaska.

DID YOU KNOW?

Aurora borealis (northern lights) can be seen an average of 243 days a year in Fairbanks, Alaska and in many other Alaskan locations. Charged electrons and protons striking the earth's upper atmosphere produce the northern lights. If you are visiting Alaska, make sure you look at the night skies to see this amazing phenomenon.

BOOKS TO DISPLAY

Painter and Ugly by Robert J. Blake. New York, NY: Philomel Books, 2011.

The Great Serum Race: Blazing the Iditarod Trail by Debbie S. Miller. New York, NY: Walker Publishing Co., 2002.

HANDS-ON PROJECT

Discover which is the longest section of the Iditarod Trail Race by graphing the distance between checkpoints.

MATERIALS NEEDED

- Maps of Northern or Southern route
- Distances of Northern or Southern route checkpoints
- Graphing paper
- Colored pencils

DIRECTIONS

1. Determine if you will be working on one graph together as a group or individually.
2. Give each child a piece of graphing paper and a copy of the Iditarod Race route listing the distance between checkpoints. Maps and checkpoint distance can be printed from http://iditarod.com/about/the-iditarod-trail/.
3. Write the names of the checkpoints across the bottom of the graph.
4. Determine how many miles each vertical block will represent: 1 mile, 5 miles, or 10 miles.
5. Rounding to the nearest whole number, graph the distance between checkpoints. If you chose each block to represent 1 mile, you will not need to round to the nearest whole number.
6. Determine which part of the trail had the greatest distance between checkpoints. Which had the smallest?

2

Grand Canyon National Park

ARIZONA

Grand Canyon
Jason Chin. New York, NY: Roaring Brook Press, 2017.

A father and daughter explore the Grand Canyon, enjoying the scenery and nature, while also imagining what the Grand Canyon was before and what may have created the fossils they discover. Pages filled with border illustrations give details about the animals, fossils, and rocks found in the Grand Canyon. Brought to life with vibrant illustrations, the book introduces the reader to this outdoor natural wonder.

Programming Tip

The Grand Canyon National Park site has a variety of short videos that explore the natural and human history of the park. These videos feature park rangers, historians, and scientists and provide a wonderful addition to any programming. Videos can be found at www.nps.gov/grca/learn/photosmultimedia/grand-canyon-in-depth.htm.

ABOUT THE GRAND CANYON NATIONAL PARK

The Grand Canyon measures over a mile deep, 277 miles long, and 18 miles wide. It was carved five- to six-million years ago by the Colorado River. Exposed canyon walls show a variety of rock types, formations, and fossils. Native Americans consider the Grand Canyon a holy site and for several thousand years made the Grand Canyon area their home, building settlements within and around the canyons and caves. The National Park Service has maintained and protected the Grand Canyon since 1919.

DID YOU KNOW?

Four Corners is the point in the Southwestern United States where Arizona, Colorado, New Mexico, and Utah meet. It is the only point in the United States where visitors can literally step on four states at once. The landmark is marked by a monument and the Navajo Nation manages the site.

BOOKS TO DISPLAY

Where Is the Grand Canyon? by Jim O'Connor. New York, NY: Grosset & Dunlap, 2015.

Big Moon Tortilla by Joy Cowley. Honesdale, PA: Boyds Mills Press, 1998.

HANDS-ON ACTIVITY

Fossils are the remains or imprints left behind from any creature or plant that was once on Earth. From fossils we discover animals and plants that may be extinct, as well as details about life on Earth. Create your own fossil to preserve your handprint or objects found in nature.

MATERIALS NEEDED

- Clay
- Wax paper
- Paper bowl
- Seashells, stones, sticks, leaves, etc.

DIRECTIONS

1. Place wax paper in paper bowl, covering bottom and sides.
2. Work clay until smooth and press into a bottom of a paper bowl, creating a layer of clay about two inches deep.
3. If making a handprint, press hand into the clay. Remove hand and allow clay to dry.
4. If making fossil prints, press leaves, seashells, or other items into the bottom of the bowl. Remove the items and allow clay to dry.
5. Once clay has dried, remove from the bowl and display your fossil.

3

Golden Gate Bridge

CALIFORNIA

Pop's Bridge
Eve Bunting. Orlando, FL: Harcourt Press, 2006.

Every afternoon, Robert and Charlie watch the construction of the Golden Gate Bridge. Each boy believes his father has the most important job on the bridge. After a tragic accident, they realize that it takes a team effort of many people working together to build the bridge. Laborers, riveters, carpenters, painters, and skywalkers all contributed to complete the bridge. In total, over 1,000 men helped to build the Golden Gate Bridge.

Programming Tip

On April 18, 1906, a significant earthquake struck the coast of Northern California and San Francisco, measuring an estimated 7.9 magnitude. As a result, fires erupted through the city and lasted for days, destroying over 80% of San Francisco. *I Survived the San Francisco Earthquake, 1906* by Lauren Tarshis is a wonderful resource to use for guided reading lessons and to learn more about the events.

ABOUT THE GOLDEN GATE BRIDGE

Open to the public since 1937, the Golden Gate Bridge connects San Francisco to Marin County, California. This suspension bridge is 1.7 miles long and 90 feet wide. While being built, divers had to plunge in the ocean to depths of 90 feet to blast away rock, remove debris, and place bridge supports. The bridge color, international orange, was chosen because it complements the green hills and blue water and makes the Golden Gate Bridge one of the most recognizable in the world. To keep the bridge its original orange color, workers repaint the bridge year-round using 10,000 gallons of paint annually.

DID YOU KNOW?

San Francisco is a peninsula surrounded by the Pacific Ocean. The area is known for its 43 hills and the last manually operated cable car system. You can learn more about San Francisco's cable cars at www.sfcablecar.com/.

BOOKS TO DISPLAY

What Was the San Francisco Earthquake? by Dorothy Hoobler. New York, NY: Grosset & Dunlap, 2016.

This Bridge Will Not Be Gray by Dave Eggers. San Francisco, CA: McSweeney's, 2015.

I Survived the San Francisco Earthquake, 1906 by Lauren Tarshis. New York, NY: Scholastic, Inc., 2012.

Fly High, Fly Low by Don Freeman. New York, NY: Viking Press, 1957.

HANDS-ON PROJECT

Suspension bridges suspend the roadway by using cables, ropes, or chains from two tall towers. The towers support the majority of the weight as compression pushes down on the bridge's deck and then travels up the cables, ropes, or chains to transfer compression to the towers. The towers then dissipate the compression directly into the earth. Show the students various pictures of suspension bridges and have them create their own bridge with a variety of household items.

MATERIALS NEEDED

- Toilet paper rolls
- Paper straws
- Scissors
- Tape

DIRECTIONS

1. Add two long straws vertically on opposite sides of a toilet paper tube. Bend top half of the straws at an angle and connect them together at the top, securing with tape. Repeat process, creating a total of 3 support structures.
2. Lay 4–5 straws side-by-side across top of tubes between the vertical straws to create a base or road. Tape in place.
3. Cut straws in half and connect them diagonally from the tops of the long vertical straws to the base of the bridge.

4

Kennedy Space Center

FLORIDA

Astronaut Handbook

Meghan McCarthy. New York, NY: Alfred A. Knopf, 2008.

Astronaut Handbook is a perfect introduction for anyone who dreams of becoming an astronaut. *Astronaut Handbook* describes the different types of astronauts and their jobs, as well as training and details of space flight. Learn how astronauts practice being weightless on the Vomit Comet, how a crumb could be dangerous, and how a space toilet works. A list of fascinating facts in the back of the book compliments the story.

ABOUT THE KENNEDY SPACE CENTER

The National Aeronautics and Space Administration (NASA) opened in October 1958, concentrating on the advancement of human and robotic spaceflight. In May 1961, President John F. Kennedy announced his goal to land a man on the moon and return him safely to earth before the end of the decade. This began the US' ambitious space race. On July 16, 1969, the Apollo 11 mission successfully launched Astronauts Neil Armstrong, Michael Collins, and Edwin "Buzz" Aldrin, Jr., from the Kennedy Space Center in Florida to the moon, where they landed on July 20, 1969. The Kennedy Space Center is the primary launch site for NASA's human spaceflight. Cape Canaveral Air Force Station is the primary launch site for robotics missions. The Kennedy Space Center is an immense complex, covering 219 square miles. Since only a small part of the area is developed, the site is also a wildlife sanctuary and home to Merritt Island National Wildlife Refuge and Canaveral National Seashore.

Did You Know?

Much of the Kennedy Space Center is restricted from the public. There is a visitor center complex and activities you can participate in with the purchase of an admissions ticket.

PROGRAMMING TIP

The International Space Station orbits around the Earth and has contributions from 15 nations, including NASA (United States), Roscosmos (Russia), and the European Space Agency. Over 230 people from 18 countries have visited the International Space Station. Astronaut Scott Kelly spent a year in space collecting data on the International Space Station. He also took photographs documenting his time in space. To see his some of his remarkable photos visit **www.nasa.gov/content/best-year-in-space-photographs-from-scott-kelly**.

To learn when the space station will by flying over your area, sign up for alerts at **https://spotthestation.nasa.gov/home.cfm**.

BOOKS TO DISPLAY

Counting on Katherine by Helaine Becker. New York, NY: Henry Holt & Co., 2018.

Eight Days Gone by Linda McReynolds. Watertown, MA: Chalesbridge, 2012.

Moonshot: The Flight of Apollo 11 by Brian Floca. New York, NY: Atheneum Books for Young Readers, 2009.

HANDS-ON PROJECT

Rockets are launched into space using great speed and energy to escape the gravitational pull from Earth. Rockets move upward by sending hot exhaust gas down, creating an equal and opposite reaction. When an equal and opposite reaction is created, scientific laws of motion that were developed by Isaac Newton are being used. The following experiments will help reinforce Newton's laws of motion.

MATERIALS NEEDED

- Rubber balloons (oblong or round)
- Binder clip
- Thin rope of cotton cooking twine
- Straws
- Tape
- Tape measure
- Two chairs, door knobs, or other supports across from each other to tie the twine to

DIRECTIONS

1. Tie one end of the twine to a chair or other support.
2. Put other end of the twine through a straw, then tie to another support at a distance of your choosing.
3. Blow up the balloon, but do not tie it. Twist the end closed and place binder clip on it so air does not release.
4. Tape the balloon to the straw along its midsection.
5. Remove the binder clip and watch the balloon fly across the string.
6. Measure the distance the balloon travelled. Repeat using different distances for the string length and blow the balloon up different amounts.
7. Discuss what amount of balloon inflation allowed the balloon to travel the greatest distance.

5

Lei Day Festival

HAWAII

Luka's Quilt

Georgia Guback. New York, NY: Greenwillow Books, 1994.

Tutu has a dream of a quilt to create for her granddaughter, Luka. When Luka sees the finished quilt, made in the Hawaiian tradition of just two colors, she is disappointed and her grandmother is hurt. After watching Luka create a lei at the Lei Day Festival, Tutu is inspired to create a colorful quilted lei to place over the traditional Hawaiian quilt.

Programming Tip

Folktales are stories passed on from one generation to another. Often told orally, they explain a people's origin or tradition. Hawaii has many folktales and creation tales, explaining the origin of people coming to the islands and their many gods who protected the land and people. *Dog-of-the-Sea-Waves* by James Rumford shares the story of the five brothers who came to explore the Hawaiian Islands. After reading the book, ask your class to create their own creation story about their family, pets, or friends. Then have them draw a picture and orally share their tale.

ABOUT THE LEI DAY FESTIVAL

Early settlers brought leis to the Hawaiian Islands and often constructed them from flowers, leaves, seeds, nuts, shells, and other items found in nature. Worn for beauty, garlands were used by tribes to distinguish themselves from each other. Leis could also signify a peace agreement between island chiefs. Held on May 1 each year, the Lei holiday began in 1928 to celebrate the Hawaiian custom of making and wearing leis. There are festivals and celebrations on each of the major Hawaiian Islands, and each island has a lei of its own with specialty flowers from the region. The lei is a symbol of welcome and great care is taken when making a lei. Once a lei is prepared, tradition states that the spirit of the lei's creator is woven into it.

DID YOU KNOW?

On December 7, 1941, Japan attacked the battleship USS Arizona at Pearl Harbor in Honolulu, Hawaii, launching the United States into World War II. Today, the National Park Service operates the USS Arizona Memorial.

BOOKS TO DISPLAY

Pig-Boy: A Trickster Tale from Hawai'i by Gerald McDermott. Orlando, FL: Harcourt, 2009.

Dog-of-the-Sea-Waves by James Rumford. Boston, MA: Houghton Mifflin Company, 2004.

Dumpling Soup by Jama Kim Rattigan. Boston, MA: Joy Street Books, 1993.

HANDS-ON PROJECT

Leis add joy to any celebration! Make and share these leis at your next gathering.

MATERIALS NEEDED

- Paper cupcake liners in a variety of colors
- Hole punch
- Straws cut to 1 1/2 inches in length
- Yarn
- Masking tape
- Scissors

DIRECTIONS

1. Cut yarn to 20 inches in length.
2. Wrap a piece of masking tape around one end of yarn to allow it to pass more easily through the cupcake liners and straws.
3. Punch a hole in the center of the cupcake liners, choosing a variety of colors.
4. Alternate threading the yarn through a cupcake liner and straw piece. When you have finished threading the flowers and straws, tie off the ends of the yarn to create a necklace lei.

6

Mardi Gras, New Orleans

LOUISIANA

A Catfish Tale: A Bayou Story of the Fisherman and His Wife
Whitney Stewart. Chicago, IL: Albert Whitman & Co., 2014.

When a fisherman encounters a magical catfish in the bayou, his wife demands he make a wish on her behalf. The wife continues to demand more and more, until eventually she wishes she were not only Queen of Mardi Gras, but also Queen of the Bayou. This book is a wonderful introduction to the culture of New Orleans and Mardi Gras.

Programming Tip

In addition to Mardi Gras, New Orleans hosts many celebrations and festivals throughout the year. One of the most well known and popular is the New Orleans Jazz and Heritage Festival, known as Jazz Fest, which encourages the promotion of music, arts, and culture of New Orleans. The festival begins in late April and runs through the first weekend in May. To experience the flavor of traditional New Orleans jazz, Preservation Hall provides sound clips at **http://preservationhall.com/hall/music/.**

ABOUT MARDI GRAS

Mardi Gras refers to Fat Tuesday, the final day of revelry before Ash Wednesday, which signifies the beginning of Lent in the Christian faith. New Orleans held its first Mardi Gras parade in 1857, beginning the tradition of a parade with floats. By law, float riders must wear masks. Float riders also throw trinkets to the crowds, most notably beads. Mardi Gras events and celebrations typically take place the week leading up to and including Fat Tuesday each year.

DID YOU KNOW?

While celebrating Mardi Gras, you may stumble upon the Mardi Gras Indians who participate in parades, but never publish their parade dates or routes. The Mardi Gras Indians are comprised mainly of African American communities who named themselves after Native American Indians. They aim to pay homage and show respect to the tribes who helped their ancestors escape slavery. The Mardi Gras Indians make elaborate costumes, rich in tradition and artistry.

BOOKS TO DISPLAY

The 5 O'Clock Band by Troy Andrews. New York, NY: Abrams Books for Young Readers, 2018.

Mardi Gras and Carnival by Molly Aloian. New York, NY: Crabtree Publishing Co., 2010.

HANDS-ON PROJECT

Mardi Gras masks were traditionally worn to allow people to celebrate in any way they wanted without being recognized. Today, people wear masks to add excitement and magic to the celebration. Create your own Mardi Gras mask and join in the celebration!

MATERIALS NEEDED

- Mask Template, printed on card stock for each student
- Crayons, markers and colored pencils as desired
- Glitter, gems, feathers and other adornments as desired
- Glue
- Scissors
- Hole punch
- Ribbon or yarn

DIRECTIONS

1. Punch holes on each side of the mask so that a ribbon or string can be added.
2. Provide each child a mask to decorate.
3. Color and decorate the mask as desired.
4. After the mask is dry, tie ribbon or yarn to each hole. The ribbon should be long enough so that you can tie the mask around the child's head.

7

Chaco Culture National Historic Park

NEW MEXICO

Carlos and the Squash Plant
Jan Romero Stevens. Flagstaff, AZ: Northland, 1993.

Carlos works on his parents' farm in New Mexico. Each day Carlos returns from the fields and his mother tells him to bathe, and each day Carlos ignores his mother's demands. Unfortunately, Carlos discovers what happens when you do not wash; a squash plant sprouts from your ear! This wonderful southwestern folktale is sprinkled throughout with Spanish phrases and images that portray the region.

ABOUT CHACO CULTURE NATIONAL HISTORIC PARK

Located in Northwestern New Mexico, the Chaco Culture National Historic Park has the largest concentration of pueblos in the American Southwest. The Chaco Canyon was a major center for Puebloan culture. Beginning in the mid-800s, people constructed massive stone buildings containing multiple stories with hundreds of rooms. The Chaco area is thought to be a gathering place where many clans converged to share their ceremonies, traditions, and knowledge. Many modern Southwest Indians trace their heritage to this Chaco culture.

Programming Tip

The Chaco Culture National Historic Park has a variety of lesson plans for students of all ages. Check out these wonderful resources for programming ideas. **www.nps.gov/chcu/learn/education/classrooms/curriculummaterials.htm.**

DID YOU KNOW?

The Indian Pueblo Cultural Center is a museum that contains the history, art and culture of the 19 Pueblos of New

Mexico. In addition to the museum exhibit, they also host a variety of events and ceremonies, including traditional Native American dances.

BOOKS TO DISPLAY

Thunder Boy Jr. by Sherman Alexie. New York, NY: Little, Brown and Co., 2016.

Welcome to Josefina's World 1824 by Yvette La Pierre. Middleton, WI: Pleasant Company Publications, 1999.

Abuelita's Heart by Amy Cordova. New York, NY: Simon & Schuster, 1997.

HANDS-ON PROJECT

Kachina dolls are traditional dolls made by the Hopi Indians. Each doll represents a spirit, deity, or natural element. Often, dolls include a chief, ceremonial dancer, the sun, or a buffalo.

MATERIALS NEEDED

- Toilet paper or other cardboard tube
- Styrofoam ball for head
- Fabric or felt
- Feathers, beads, or other decorative items
- Paint or markers
- Glue
- Tape
- Scissors

DIRECTIONS

1. Using hot glue or a quick drying glue, attach the Styrofoam ball to the top of the cardboard tube and allow time to completely dry.
2. Add facial details with markers or paint.
3. Create clothes with fabric, colored papers, paint or markers.
4. Add decorative details with beads, feathers, buttons, ribbon, and other materials.

8

Statue of Liberty

NEW YORK

Why Is the Statue of Liberty Green?
Martha E. H. Rustad. Minneapolis, MN: Millbrook Press, 2015.

When a class goes on a fieldtrip to Liberty Island, they learn the history of the Statue of Liberty and discover why she is green. This book is the perfect introduction to how and why the Statue of Liberty was built, and what the gift meant to both the American and French people.

ABOUT THE STATUE OF LIBERTY

In anticipation of America's 100th birthday since the signing of the Declaration of Independence on July 4, 1776, Edouard de Laboulaye wanted to celebrate with a spectacular gift from the French people, the Statue of Liberty. In order to complete such a task, he solicited donations from both the French and American people so that the Statue would be a gift from one people to another and a symbol of freedom. Frederic-Auguste Bartholdi was the architect employed to design and build the Statue. Constructed in France, the Statue of Liberty was taken apart and shipped to America as 350 pieces in 214 crates. It then took 4 months to reassemble the Statue on a pedestal base built in America with funds raised by the American people. The Statue of Liberty was unveiled on October 28, 1886. The entire structure stands 305 feet tall, with the Statue of Liberty being 151 feet. The Statue of Liberty greeted millions of immigrants as they passed through Ellis Island when coming to America between 1892–1954.

Programming Tip

Have you ever wondered what the view from the crown of the Statue of Liberty would be like? Visit the official National Park Service webcams to see what Lady Liberty is looking at! You can also get a view of her. **www.nps.gov/stli/learn/photosmultimedia/webcams.htm**

DID YOU KNOW?

Before the Statue of Liberty's creation, the area was actually home to Fort Wood, a stone fort constructed in 1807. Located in the harbor, Fort Wood was an ideal position to defend New York. When visiting Liberty Island, take time to explore the remnants of Fort Wood and the National Park Service exhibits.

BOOKS TO DISPLAY

Blue Sky White Stars by Sarvinder Naberhaus. New York, NY: Dial Books for Young Readers, 2017.

Liberty Rising: The Story of the Statue of Liberty by Pegi Deitz Shea. New York, NY: Henry Holt and Company, 2005.

HANDS-ON PROJECT

The Statue of Liberty is a great feat of engineering. Building a stable structure that stands tall utilizes many engineering skills, such as understanding the distribution of mass and the concepts of compression and tension. Using standard spaghetti and marshmallows, children can practice these concepts while creating their own tower.

MATERIALS NEEDED

- Spaghetti (straws are an alternative.)
- Marshmallows
- Yard stick or measuring tape

DIRECTIONS

1. Determine how much time you want to give the children to complete their tower and if they will be working alone or in small groups.
2. Suggest to the children that they create a sturdy base to support the structure as it becomes taller. In addition, the spaghetti can be broken in half to create a shorter distance between connector marshmallows if children feel that would work best in their structure.
3. Give each child/group spaghetti and marshmallows. You will need to determine if you want each group to work with a certain amount of spaghetti and marshmallows, or if they have unlimited resources.
4. Have the children create a stable structure.
5. At the end of the building time, measure the structures and see which is the tallest. Discuss what made the tallest structure the most stable.

9

Oregon Trail

MISSOURI TO OREGON

Papa and the Pioneer Quilt
Jean Van Leeuwen. New York, NY: Dial Book for Young Readers, 2007.

Rebecca and her family leave all they know behind and set out west for the promise of a better life in Oregon. Along the way, they cross wide prairies, rivers, and mountains and meet wonderful people following the same trail to this new land. As they walk thousands of miles with other families, Rebecca begins collecting scraps of fabric left from her adventures on the trail, eventually having enough pieces to make a quilt decorated with the "Wandering Foot" pattern.

Programming Tip

The National Historic Trail Interpretive Center provides Oregon Trail Journey lesson plans. They include supply information, writing prompts, and packing list activities. Make use of this resource at **www.blm.gov/or/oregontrail/files/packwagon.pdf.**

ABOUT THE OREGON TRAIL

The Oregon Trail began in Independence, Missouri and ended in "Oregon Country," which consisted of present-day Oregon, Washington, Idaho, and parts of Montana and Wyoming. From the 1830s–1860s, thousands of families travelled across the plains carrying their belongings in wagons. Anything that could not be carried or fit in the wagon was sold or left behind. Free fertile farmland was promised to each head of household who settled in Oregon, and married couples could claim up to 640 acres at no cost. People often walked 15 miles per day in order to get to Oregon before winter. After 1869, the Central and Union Pacific Railroad began running trips west, essentially ending the foot and wagon travel across the Trail. Instead of traveling for 6 months, the train trip took one week.

DID YOU KNOW?

The Gateway Arch Monument in St. Louis, Missouri, opened in 1965. The 630-foot monument was built to recognize the Westward Expansion of the United States. A visit to the museum at Gateway Arch provides information on Thomas Jefferson's role in opening the West, the pioneers who made the decision to travel West, and important court cases for African Americans.

BOOKS TO DISPLAY

Voices from the Oregon Trail by Kay Winters. New York, NY: Dial Books for Young Readers, 2014.

Your Life as a Pioneer on the Oregon Trail by Jessica Gunderson. North Mankato, MN: Picture Window Books, 2012.

Journey of a Pioneer by Patricia Murphy. New York, NY: DK Publishing, 2008.

HANDS-ON PROJECT

Travelling along the Oregon Trail was frequently a group effort. Families came together to travel and selected a wagon master to lead them on their journey west. Wagon trains were often 3 miles long. Prepare for the journey west together as a class, in smaller groups, or individually. Wagons, Ho!

MATERIALS NEEDED

- Map of the Oregon Trail (there are a variety available online)
- Pencil
- Paper

DIRECTIONS

1. Make a list of items that you own. Think of the electronics, games, clothing, books, toys, and sports equipment you own.
2. Make a list of all the essential items you need each day to live. What personal products do you use each day? How much food and water do you consume?
3. Look at your lists and think about what you could actually fit in your wagon or car if you were traveling the Oregon Trail. Remember, there are no restaurants or hotels to stop at along the way. What items on your list are essential? Cross the items off your list that you would need to leave behind.
4. Which is the hardest item for you to leave behind? Write a paragraph telling why the item needs to be left behind and why it is the most difficult item for you to leave.

10

The Liberty Bell and Independence National Historic Park

PENNSYLVANIA

Saving the Liberty Bell

Marty Rhodes Figley. Minneapolis, MN: Millbrook Press, 2005.

Saving the Liberty Bell tells the story of John Mickley and his son Johnny, who escaped Philadelphia with the Liberty Bell in their wagon during the American Revolution. The British were about to attack Philadelphia and intended to melt all the bronze bells to turn them into ammunition. Farmers were asked to take all the bells to safe hiding places outside of Philadelphia. John and his son were in charge of delivering the Liberty Bell to its hiding place in a church several miles outside of town.

Programming Tip

The National Park Service provides lesson plans for the Liberty Bell and Independence National Historic Park for all ages. Visit the website to learn more about their wonderful resources. **www.nps.gov/inde/learn/education/classrooms/curriculummaterials.htm.** If you want to hear the Liberty Bell, you can listen to a sound clip at **www.nps.gov/inde/photosmultimedia-soundofthelibertybell.htm.**

ABOUT THE LIBERTY BELL AND INDEPENDENCE NATIONAL HISTORIC PARK

Philadelphia was the center of power for the newly formed United States. Both the Declaration of Independence and the US Constitution were signed inside Independence Hall. The Liberty Bell, a symbol of freedom and liberty for the United States, is located nearby. These sites are open to the public and allow you to get a glimpse at what life was like during revolutionary times.

DID YOU KNOW?

Independence National Historic Park includes the Liberty Bell Center, Independence Hall, Congress Hall, the National Constitution Center, and the Benjamin Franklin Museum. Tickets are required to tour Independence Hall.

BOOKS TO DISPLAY

Mrs. Millie Goes to Philly! by Judy Cox. Tarrytown, NY: Marshall Cavendish Corporation, 2008.

Saving the Liberty Bell by Megan McDonald. New York, NY: Atheneum Books, 2005.

HANDS-ON PROJECT

In 1880, John Phillip Sousa was named the director of the US Marine Band, a position he held for 12 years. Later, he formed his own band, the New Marine Band. Sousa is a well-known composer of many marches often played at patriotic events. One of his most recognizable patriotic marches is "The Stars and Stripes Forever."

Offer this program near the Fourth of July to celebrate Independence Day. Create rhythm shakers, play traditional Sousa patriotic marches, carry red, white, and blue streamers, and have your own parade down the sidewalk or around the classroom.

MATERIALS NEEDED

- Paper towel or toilet paper cardboard tubes
- Thin paper plates
- Rice, beans, bells, or other items that can fit inside the tube
- Wax paper or plastic wrap
- Rubber bands
- Stapler/staples
- Crayons, markers, stickers, and other decorating items

DIRECTIONS

1. Choose a cardboard tube or paper plate to decorate. If you choose a paper plate, you will need to decorate the bottom of the plate as it will be folded, filled with a noise item, and stapled closed.
2. If you have a tube, cover one end with a square of wax paper or plastic wrap and secure with a rubber band. If you have a plate, fold in half.
3. Fill the tube or plate with rice, beans, or other noise-making items.
4. If you have a tube, cover other end with square of wax paper or plastic wrap and secure with a rubber band. If you have a plate, staple along the folded edges so that noise items cannot slip out.
5. Shake your noisemaker as you march and dance!

11

Mount Rushmore National Memorial

SOUTH DAKOTA

Hanging off Jefferson's Nose: Growing Up on Mount Rushmore

Tina Nichols Coury. New York, NY: Dial Books for Young Readers, 2012.

Hanging off Jefferson's Nose details the story of Gutzon Borglum and his son Lincoln as they honor the great presidents who shaped the nation by carving Mount Rushmore. Located in the Black Hills of South Dakota, the project officially began on August 10, 1927. During the many years it took to carve the monument, Gutzon Borglum passed away, leaving his son Lincoln to complete the project in 1944.

Programming Tip

Mount Rushmore National Memorial has a variety of lesson plans for students of all ages. Check out these wonderful resources for programming ideas. **www.nps.gov/moru/learn/education/classrooms/curriculum materials.htm.**

ABOUT MOUNT RUSHMORE NATIONAL MEMORIAL

In the Black Hills of South Dakota, Mount Rushmore features 60-foot high carvings of George Washington, Thomas Jefferson, Abraham Lincoln, and Theodore Roosevelt. The sculptor, Gutzon Borglum, created the design and oversaw the project with the assistance of his son Lincoln and over 400 workers. At the time, Gutzon Borglum felt these presidents represented the most important events in the history of the United States. George Washington led the colonists during the American Revolutionary War and was the first president of the United States. Thomas Jefferson was the primary author of the Declaration of Independence and he purchased the Louisiana Territory, which doubled the size of our country. Abraham Lincoln preserved the union of our country during the Civil War. Theodore Roosevelt provided leadership during America's economic growth, negotiated construction of the Panama Canal, and fought to ensure the rights of workers.

DID YOU KNOW?

Mount Rushmore is only a small part of the 1.25-million-acre Black Hills National Forest. In addition to the prairie grasslands and forests, a massive cave system also exists. Wind Cave National Park is known for its winds at the cave's entrance and its abundant boxwork calcite formations. The cave consists of 140 miles of explored cave passageways.

BOOKS TO DISPLAY

Where Is Mount Rushmore? by True Kelley. New York, NY: Grosset & Dunlap, 2015.

A T.Rex Named Sue: Sue Hendrickson's Huge Discovery by Natalie Lunis. New York, NY: Bearport Publishing Co., 2007.

HANDS-ON PROJECT

Sculpting takes time and patience. Practice creating your own image.

MATERIALS NEEDED

- Table coverings
- 1–2 pounds of clay per person, moldable modeling clay or play-doh.
- Carving tools, plastic utensils will work well
- Water if using clay
- Mirror

DIRECTIONS

1. Study yourself in a mirror. Notice the shape of your eyes, nose, and mouth. Notice the texture of your hair.
2. Shape the clay into a square or rectangle. Begin carving sections of your image into the clay.
3. Once you are satisfied with the image, allow the clay to dry.

12

Vaqueros and American Cowboys

TEXAS

Armadillo Rodeo

Jan Brett. New York, NY: Putnam's Sons, 1995.

The day Harmony Jean wears her brand-new chili-pepper-red cowboy boots, Bo, the armadillo, is sure he spots a red armadillo across the creek. Before Bo can catch up to the red armadillo, it is suddenly on the move. Bo's adventure leads him to the Curly H Rodeo, where he gets to do all the things he has dreamed of doing, including dancing the two-step. Jan Brett's vibrant illustrations enhance the story, and the intricate border illustrations add detail and foretell future action.

ABOUT VAQUEROS AND AMERICAN COWBOYS

The Spanish arrived in the Americas in the 1500's. Soon after their arrival, ranches were built to raise cattle, and horses were imported from Spain to work on the ranch. Vaqueros, known for their superior roping, riding, and herding skills, were hired by ranchers to tend the livestock. By the 1700s, ranching was a way of life in Texas. With the Westward Expansion in the 1800s, many English-speaking settlers adopted the clothing and cattle driving methods of the vaquero culture. Cowboys were responsible for herding livestock, caring for horses, and repairing fences and buildings. Cowboys often tested their skills against one another by performing in rodeos. These competitions included bull riding, calf roping, steer wrestling, bareback bronco riding, and barrel racing.

Programming Tip

Jan Brett's website has a variety of activities to enhance her books. Make use of this wonderful resource at **www.janbrett.com/index.html.**

DID YOU KNOW?

On September 8, 1900, a Category 4 hurricane made landfall in the city of Galveston, Texas. A 15-foot storm surge flooded the city, making it the deadliest natural disaster in the history of the United States. *Texas: A Nonfiction Companion to Magic Tree House #30: Hurricane Heroes in Texas* by Mary Pope Osborne provides information on this event and is a welcome addition to any hurricane science programming.

BOOKS TO DISPLAY

Texas: A Nonfiction Companion to Magic Tree House #30: Hurricane Heroes in Texas by Mary Pope Osborne. New York, NY: Random House Books for Young Readers, 2018.

Meanwhile, Back at the Ranch by Anne Isaacs. New York, NY: Schwartz & Wade, 2014.

Bubba, the Cowboy Prince: A Fractured Texas Tale by Helen Ketteman. New York, NY: Scholastic Press, 1997.

HANDS-ON PROJECT

Cowboys spent long days working on the ranch or herding cattle. In the evening, they gathered around a campfire to tell stories. Often, cowboys could not read or write, so they would memorize their favorite stories to share later. Many of these stories, known as cowboy poems, rhymed to make them easier to memorize. Cowboys also would sing to keep the herds from stampeding, creating cowboy songs. Sometimes the stories and songs would tell of daring adventures from their day. Think about a day that you had a daring adventure. Write your own story, poem, or song retelling your tale.

13

The White House

WASHINGTON, D.C.

When Penny Met POTUS
Rachel Ruiz. New York, NY: Picture Window Books, 2016.

Penny's mom works in a large white house for someone named POTUS. When Penny goes to work with her mom, she imagines who POTUS could be. Could POTUS be a space creature? As Penny searches the White House for the mysterious POTUS, she is a little disappointed to discover POTUS is not the special creature she had imagined. However, she soon discovers that POTUS is a lot like her.

Programming Tip

Established in 1846, The Smithsonian Institution consists of a group of museums and research centers administered by the US government that are free and fully accessible to the public. Regardless of your area of interest, there are museums, galleries, gardens, and a zoo for you to visit. If you cannot go to the sites in person, visit the website for educational materials available online at **www.si.edu.**

ABOUT THE WHITE HOUSE

George Washington, the first president of the United States, selected the site where the White House would be built in 1791. In 1800, President John Adams and his wife, Abigail, were the first people to live in the unfinished house. Over the years, many updates and additions have been made to the White House. Washington D.C. is actually not part of any state; instead, it's an independent federal district situated between the states of Maryland and Virginia overlooking the Potomac River. The White House and Washington, D.C. represent the center of democracy and the central government in the United States. The government of the United States is made up of three branches: the executive branch, the legislative branch, and the judicial branch. The president, who is elected by the people every 4 years, leads the executive branch. The president has many powers, including the ability to sign legislation into law or veto bills, as well as negotiate and sign treaties with other nations.

DID YOU KNOW?

If you would like to visit the White House, you must request a visit through your Congressional representative. If you are not a citizen, you can make arrangements through your embassy.

BOOKS TO DISPLAY

The House That George Built by Suzanne Slade. Watertown, MA: Charlesbridge, 2012.

Madam President by Lane Smith. New York, NY: Hyperion Books, 2008.

HANDS-ON PROJECT

The President of the United States is an important position to hold in the United States government. Ask the children: what types of education, experience, and training are needed to be president? What qualities do you think a person needs to be a good president? Read *Madam President* by Lane Smith and have the children discuss and write what they would do if they were president and why.

PART II

Exploring Other Countries

14

San People, Formerly Known as the Bushmen of South Africa

BOTSWANA, AFRICA

Ostrich and Lark
Marilyn Nelson. Honesdale, PA: Boyds Mills Press, Inc. 2012.

Ostrich and Lark spend each day together, with Lark singing and Ostrich silent. In the evening, Lark returns to his hidden nest and Ostrich tucks his head under a wing to go to sleep. Each day is the same until, one evening, Ostrich fluttered his billowy wings, stretched his neck, and made a booming noise! Ostrich was so loud, he boomed Lark right off his perch. This delightful tale is enhanced with illustrations that were created by the San artists as part of the Kuru Art Project in Botswana.

Programming Tip

Share *Honey . . . Honey . . . Lion!* by Jan Brett with your class and visit her website to watch a short video documenting her trip to Botswana and her encounters with some amazing animals. **www.janbrettvideos.com/african_safairi_high_bandwidth.htm**

ABOUT THE SAN PEOPLE

The San people, formerly known as the Bushmen, are the oldest inhabitants of southern Africa. The San are thought to be descendants of Early Stone Age ancestors. Rock paintings dating back 26,000 years have been found in South Africa and give clues about the San's social customs and belief systems. Today, descendants of these first people create art to share their life experiences, traditions, and the loss of their hunter-gatherer existence. Established in 1990, the Kuru Art Project allows artists to create art that continues their ancestors' tradition.

DID YOU KNOW?

Chobe National Park is Botswana's first national park and is home to Africa's largest elephant population, an estimated 120,000. Diverse wildlife includes buffalo, lions, leopards, and a variety of birds. The first inhabitants of this area were descended from the San Bushmen, and their rock paintings can still be found in the park.

BOOKS TO DISPLAY

Meerkat Mail by Emily Gravett. New York, NY: Simon & Schuster Books for Young Readers, 2007.

Honey...Honey...Lion! by Jan Brett. New York, NY: G.P. Putnam's Sons, 2005.

HANDS-ON PROJECT

The San people's rock art is found primarily in caves and rock shelters. Images often depict their beliefs and events in their daily lives. Show the class cave and rock drawings that have been discovered. Create your own rock drawing showing animals you own or love. Add your lasting signature with your handprint.

MATERIALS NEEDED

- Brown grocery bags or butcher paper
- Colored chalks, pastels, or crayons

DIRECTIONS

1. Give each child a large piece of brown paper. Have them crinkle it to create a rough, weathered, stone-like appearance.
2. Using neutral colors, draw animals of your choice.
3. Add your handprint on the paper.

15

Aborigines Indigenous People

AUSTRALIA

Possum Magic

Mem Fox. San Diego, CA: Harcourt Brace Jovanovich, 1983.

Grandma Poss's magic turns Hush invisible, leaving her safe to play with and near many of the animals found in Australia. However, when Hush decides she wants to see herself again, it is up to Grandma Poss to help. Hush and Grandma set off on an adventure around Australia, exploring the country and tasting regional foods that have the power to make Hush visible again.

ABOUT THE ABORIGINES

Aborigines are Australia's first people who are believed to be direct descendants of migrants from Asia over 50,000 years ago. Today, Aborigines make up 2% of Australia's population and primarily live in the desert areas of the Australian outback. Ubirr, a group of rock outcrops, served as Aboriginal rock shelters. The rock shelters were a canvas for the Aboriginal people, illustrated with drawings from their everyday life. The shelters provide a detailed record with stories of creation and animals and traditional food illustrated. Some paintings are 20,000 years old. Much of the Ubirr rock outcrop is part of Kakadu National park.

Programming Tip

The Great Barrier Reef Marine Park website provides information and a short introduction video on the reef to share with the class.
www.gbrmpa.gov.au

DID YOU KNOW?

Comprised of nearly 3,000 separate reefs and more than 900 tropical islands, the Great Barrier Reef stretches over 1,200 miles. The Great Barrier Reef contains 400 types of coral,

1,500 species of fish, and 4,000 types of mollusk. The Great Barrier Reef is one of the Seven Natural Wonders of the World.

BOOKS TO DISPLAY

Over in Australia: Amazing Animals Down Under by Marianne Collins Berkes. Nevada City, CA: Dawn Publications, 2011.

Diary of a Baby Wombat by Jackie French. Boston, MA: Clarion Books, 2010.

The Biggest Frog in Australia by Susan L. Roth. New York, NY: Simon and Schuster, 1996.

HANDS-ON PROJECT

Created with a hollow wooden branch and dipped in beeswax to make a mouthpiece, a didgeridoo is a long wooden trumpet-like instrument used by the Aboriginal people of Australia to make music.

MATERIALS NEEDED

- Wrapping paper cardboard tube, or 2 paper towel cardboard tubes taped together
- Paint, markers, or crayons
- String, yarn, or twine
- Feathers
- Beads
- Glue

DIRECTIONS

1. Use the internet to show your class images of a didgeridoo. You can also search for Australian Aboriginal people art symbols to give the students ideas for decorating their didgeridoo.
2. Using paint, markers, or crayons, decorate the cardboard tube with bright colors.
3. Add string, feathers, beads, or other items to decorate the tube.
4. If you choose to create a mouthpiece, roll a piece of cardstock into a cone and secure it with tape or glue to the end of the tube.

16

Amazon Rainforest

BRAZIL

The Rainforest Grew All Around

Susan Mitchell. Mount Pleasant, SC: Sylvan Dell Pub., 2007.

In this adaptation of the song, "The Green Grass Grew All Around," rainforest plants, animals, and insects are introduced. From the forest floor to the top canopy, the rainforest is explored and explained. Sidebars include in-depth information about the various plants and animals introduced through text and vibrant illustrations. The end of the book includes easy classroom extension projects and activities to enhance learning.

ABOUT THE AMAZON RAINFOREST

The Amazon Rainforest is a moist broadleaf forest, primarily located in Brazil, extending to Peru, Colombia, and other South American countries. The landscape contains 1.4 billion acres of dense forests, which is half of the planet's remaining tropical forests. The Amazon Rainforest is almost as large as the continental United States. It receives between 70–100 inches of rain each year. The rainforest is valuable for the oxygen that it provides the earth and the carbon dioxide that it consumes. The Amazon Rainforest is home to 30 million people, including tribes of indigenous people, and 1 in 10 known species on earth.

Programming Tip

Read *The Umbrella* by Jan Brett to introduce children to the wonder of the Amazon Rainforest. Visit Jan Brett's website for a variety of activities to enhance her books. **www.janbrett.com/index.html**

DID YOU KNOW?

Rio de Janeiro's carnival is known throughout the world and is one of the largest celebrated festivals. The annual carnival celebration takes place between the Friday before Ash Wednesday and Ash Wednesday at noon, which marks the beginning of Lent. In the Christian faith, Lent is the forty days prior to Easter. Rio de Janerio's Carnival features more than 100 block parades, many of which are supported by the students and staff of the city's samba schools. The Carnival began in the 1830s as a continuation of the Portuguese tradition of celebrating and indulging on the day before Lent begins. During the late 1800s, street musicians and dancing were introduced in addition to themed costumes and the tradition of electing a Carnival "king."

BOOKS TO DISPLAY

The Umbrella by Jan Brett. New York, NY: G.P. Putnam's Sons, 2004.

"Slowly, Slowly, Slowly," Said the Sloth by Eric Carle. New York, NY: Philomel Books, 2002.

The Great Kapok Tree: A Tale of the Amazon Rain Forest by Lynne Cherry. San Diego, CA: Harcourt Brace Jovanovich, 1990.

HANDS-ON PROJECT

A terrarium is a unique environment for growing plants. Heat and light enter the glass container and moisture in the air condenses on the glass walls. Moisture then returns to the soil and is absorbed by the plant's roots. Create your own ecosystem with a Mason jar terrarium.

MATERIALS NEEDED

- Mason jar or other clean recycled jar
- Small plants like succulents work well, as they need little water or maintenance
- Potting soil
- Pebbles
- Small rocks
- Sand
- Moss, often found growing in shady spots in your own yard

DIRECTIONS

1. Add a drainage layer of small rocks to the bottom of the jar, about 1-1 ½ inches deep.
2. Add a layer of moss on top of the rocks, about 1-1 ½ inches deep.
3. Add a layer of pebbles on top of the moss, about 1-1 ½ inches deep.
4. Add 1-2 inches of soil on top of the pebbles.
5. Dig a small hole in the soil and add your plant.
6. Add a final layer of moss around the plant.
7. Water the moss.
8. Display in a well-lit area and water as needed.

17

Moon Festival

CHINA

Lin Yi's Lantern: A Moon Festival Tale

Brenda Williams. Cambridge, MA: Barefoot Books, 2009.

Lin Yi's mother sends him to the market to buy items for the family's moon festival picnic. More than anything, Lin Yi wants to buy a red rabbit lantern for the festival. His mother does not have any extra money, but she tells Lin Yi if he manages to bargain for the picnic items well and has money left over, he can purchase the lantern. As the family climbs the mountain that evening, the magic of the moon festival and Moon Fairy is revealed. Vibrant gouache illustrations demonstrate the bustle of the market and the enchantment of the moon festival.

Programming Tip

Moonbeams, Dumplings, and Dragon Boats: A Treasury of Chinese Holiday Tales, Activities, and Recipes by Nina Simonds is a wonderful resource to enhance programming throughout the year. Each Chinese celebration features a story to read aloud, followed by activities and recipes to try at home or in your classroom.

ABOUT THE MOON FESTIVAL

The Mid-Autumn Moon Festival has been celebrated for over 3,000 years. According to legend, at one time there were ten suns in our sky. To save the people, an archer shot down all but one sun and was rewarded with an immortality potion. He left this potion with his wife to protect, but when a thief attempted to steal it, the wife drank the potion and flew to the moon where her only companion was Jade Rabbit. Each year on the night of the moon festival, she grants the wishes of those who ask. Moon cakes are shared during the festival, traditionally stuffed with a paste made from lotus seeds or beans. Reportedly, in the 14th century, Han rebels smuggled written instructions into moon cakes on the night of the Moon Festival when they overthrew the Mongolian empire in China.

DID YOU KNOW?

With a total length of 13,170 miles and an average height of 20 to 23 feet, the Great Wall of China is a feat of human engineering. The Great Wall was constructed under many dynasties and took over 2,000 years to complete. In 220 BC, during the Qin Dynasty, sections of earlier fortifications were joined together to create a united defense system to protect territorial borders. The Great Wall was an integrated military defensive system with watchtowers for surveillance, fortresses for command posts, and towers for communications. The Great Wall of China is one of the Seven Wonders of the Modern World.

BOOKS TO DISPLAY

Thanking the Moon: Celebrating the Mid-Autumn Moon Festival by Grace Lin. New York, NY: Alfred A. Knopf, 2010.

Awakening the Dragon: The Dragon Boat Festival by Arlene Chan. Plattsburgh, NY: Tundra Books, 2004.

The Moon Lady by Amy Tan. New York: Aladdin, 1995.

HANDS-ON PROJECT

Experience the magic of the Moon Festival with your own nighttime picnic and lantern.

MATERIALS NEEDED

- Tracing paper
- Pencil
- Colored pencils
- Tape
- Hole punch
- Glow necklace or small glow stick, color of your choice
- Cord from glow stick package or piece of yarn
- Printed pictures of rabbits to trace

DIRECTIONS

1. Fold your tracing paper in half, with the closed seam at the bottom.
2. Unfold the tracing paper, noting that one-half of the paper will be the front and the other will be the back of your lantern.
3. Place the printed rabbit pictures under your tracing paper, and copy rabbits onto your tracing paper.
4. Decorate the rabbits with colored pencils.
5. Fold tracing paper in half and seal the sides with tape.
6. Punch a hole in the top center of your lantern.
7. Place a glow stick or glow necklace inside your lantern.
8. Thread the cord or yarn through the hole so that you can hold or hang your lantern.

18

Son Cubano Music

CUBA

All the Way to Havana

Margarita Engle. New York, NY: Henry Holt and Co., 2017.

When a boy and his family journey to Havana, Cara Cara, the family's blue 1954 Chevy, adds to the sounds of Cuban life. Cara Cara needs to be tinkered with daily to ensure that she will keep running. In Cuba, many of the cars are so old that you can no longer get original parts. People creatively keep their cars running, often for decades. Cara Cara's rhythmic puttering, along with other cars, musicians, and neighbors add to the sounds of the streets. Vibrant illustrations of enhanced car details and stunning cityscapes bring the colors of Cuba to life.

Programming Tip

Cubans know how to keep their cars running for decades. Challenge your class with a simple car race to test their engineering skills. Lego provides instructions on how to host your own car race, using Lego parts and a balloon! **www.lego.com/es-es/family/articles/create-your-own-lego-balloon-car-party-game-5e95c3166bc5455da3b61edfd61d0b00.**

ABOUT SON CUBANO MUSIC

The mix of cultures in Cuba has resulted in lasting musical traditions. The combination of Spanish verse and chorus, along with African vocals and drumming, led to a musical form called "Son." Son Cubano combines classical Spanish guitar with African traditions of clave rhythm, call and response structure, and percussion. Claves are a pair of wooden sticks struck together that produce a sound louder than all other instruments. Claves are the key to keeping the rhythm of Son Cubano, as well as directing dancers' footsteps. Salsa, Rumba, Bolero, and many other musical forms have descended from Son.

DID YOU KNOW?

Founded by the Spanish in 1519, Old Havana was one of the main shipping ports and shipbuilding centers. Narrow streets and much of the original architecture remain, including heavily fortified walls that protected the city.

BOOKS TO DISPLAY

Martina the Beautiful Cockroach: A Cuban Folktale by Carmen Agra Deedy. Atlanta, GA: Peachtree Publishers, 2007.

Kallaloo! by David Gershator. Tarrytown, NY: Marshall Cavendish, 2005.

The Bossy Gallito: A Traditional Cuban Folktale by Lucia M. Gonzalez. New York, NY: Scholastic, 1994.

HANDS-ON PROJECT

Music and dancing are fundamental to Cuban traditions. With the rise of Son Cubano, percussion instruments keep the rhythm of the music and dancers. Create your own percussion sections with handmade drums from simple household materials.

MATERIALS NEEDED

- Recycled metal cans, cleaned thoroughly
- Recycled oatmeal or other cylindrical containers
- Washi tape
- Construction paper
- Tape
- Glue
- Ribbon
- Markers
- Balloons
- Scissors

DIRECTIONS

1. Select a clean container to use as your drum.
2. Cut construction paper to fit the outside of your container and secure with glue or tape to cover the container.
3. Cut off the bottom of the balloon (the area you would blow into).
4. Add a small amount of glue to the top inch of the open end of the container.
5. Stretch the balloon and secure over the open end of your container. Allow to dry.
6. Add washi tape to secure and hide the edge of the balloon with a decorative border.
7. Decorate your drum as desired with washi tape, markers, ribbons or other items.

19

Eiffel Tower

FRANCE

A Walk in Paris

Salvatore Rubbino. Somerville, MA: Candlewick Press, 2014.

A girl and her grandfather explore the sites of Paris, from the fresh food markets to the Eiffel Tower. Each page continues the story of their exploration of Paris, with small factual text interwoven with the illustrations to add details about the landmarks. *A Walk in Paris* includes all the sites and flare that you associate with this amazing city.

ABOUT THE EIFFEL TOWER

Named after the engineer Gustave Eiffel, the Eiffel Tower is 1,063 feet from its base to its tip. Often thought of as the symbol that represents Paris, the Eiffel Tower is a wrought iron lattice tower located on the Champ de Mars. Construction began in January of 1887 and was completed in time for the World's Fair in Paris in 1889. Weather can affect the Eiffel Tower. It can actually grow taller or shorter by up to 6 inches depending on the temperature and sway a little in strong winds. The Eiffel Tower weighs 10,100 tons.

Programming Tip

The official Eiffel Tower website contains a Teachers Kit with activities to share with your classroom. Resources can be found at **www.toureiffel.paris/en/teachers/teacher-kit.**

DID YOU KNOW?

The most visited museum in Paris is the Louvre. The main entrance to the Louvre is through a glass pyramid. After entering the pyramid, visitors go downstairs to a hall and choose which building to enter from underground. The Louvre is home to the famous painting, "Mona Lisa," painted by Leonardo da Vinci in 1503. The museum contains over 35,000 works of art and over 380,000 objects.

BOOKS TO DISPLAY

Madame Martine by Sarah Brannen. Chicago, IL: Albert Whitman & Co, 2014.

Everybody Bonjours! by Leslie Kimmelman. New York, NY: Alfred A. Knopf, 2008.

Adele and Simon by Barbara McClintock. New York, NY: Farrar, Straus and Giroux, 2006.

Crepes by Suzette by Monica Wellington. New York, NY: Dutton Children's Books, 2004.

HANDS-ON PROJECT

Building the Eiffel Tower was an amazing accomplishment. Practice your own building skills with this tower activity. Participants can work alone or in groups. However, the only thing students can work with is regular copy paper and their ingenuity: no tape, glue, paper fasteners, or paper clips.

MATERIALS NEEDED

- 20 Sheets of 8 ½ x 11 copy paper. Copy paper can be torn, folded, cut, rolled, wadded, or manipulated in any way students choose.

DIRECTIONS

1. Instruct students that they are to build a tower that must stand on its own without being supported by anything or anyone. The tower can be built from the floor or a table.
2. Allow 5-10 minutes for the students to think about the best way to construct the tower before they begin construction. If they are working in groups, students should use this time to discuss their ideas.
3. Set a time limit for the students to construct the tower.
4. Alert students at the 5-minute and 1-minute mark prior to the end of construction and count down the last 30 seconds.
5. Instruct students to step away and then measure each structure.
6. Have the students discuss how they constructed their tower and what new ideas they have from seeing the other projects. Why did some towers stand and others not?

20

Holi Festival

INDIA

Festival of Colors
Kabir Sehgal. New York, NY: Simon and Schuster, 2018.

Signs of spring are abundant, and a family is excited as Holi is almost here. A brother and sister prepare for Holi by gathering brightly colored flowers, allowing them to dry, and then grinding the flowers into colorful powders. On the day of the Holi festival, the community dresses in white and dances in the streets, celebrating and spreading the colorful powders throughout the neighborhood.

Programming Tip

Offer your own Holi celebration in the month of March. Non-toxic Holi color powder is available at many stores and online. Make sure to tell participants to wear light colored or white clothing that can be stained, as not all the colors will wash out easily. Ideally, the entire program should be offered outside. Turn on lively music and throw the colored powder in the air for participants to dance through. A non-messy alternative is to dance with brightly colored scarves and toss about silk flowers and balloons.

ABOUT THE HOLI FESTIVAL

Holi, also called the Festival of Colors, is primarily celebrated in India after the full moon in March of each year. The Festival marks the end of winter and the abundance of the upcoming spring season and commemorates the victory of good over evil. The festival begins with an evening bonfire. The next morning, colored powders and colored water are thrown about, adding rainbows of color to people dressed in white clothing. Traditionally, the colored powders were made by drying and grinding flower petals. Now, most people buy premade color powders. Unlike other festivals in India, Holi is not a religious festival; it is simply a day for having fun.

DID YOU KNOW?

Three million people visit the Taj Mahal each year. The Taj Mahal is an immense mausoleum constructed of white marble, built in Agra between 1631 and 1648 by order of the Mughal emperor Shah Jahan in memory of his favorite wife. The shimmering white marble appears to change color depending on the daylight. It is inlaid with semi-precious stones that form intricate designs in a technique known as pietra dura. The Taj Mahal is enhanced with minarets, tall slender towers, which provide a focal point and are traditionally used for the Muslim call to prayer. The Taj Mahal is a lasting example of Muslim art in India.

BOOKS TO DISPLAY

Nabeel's New Pants: An Eid Tale by Fawzia Gilani-Williams. Tarrytown, NY: Marshall Cavendish Children, 2010.

Mama's Saris by Pooja Makhijani. New York, NY: Little, Brown, & Co., 2007.

HANDS-ON PROJECT

The Taj Mahal's intricate designs are made from semi-precious stones, including jade, crystal, lapis lazuli, amethyst, and turquoise. This technique is known as pietra dura, where colored stones are cut and fit together to create images. Create your own Taj Mahal with recycled boxes and colored paper gems.

MATERIALS NEEDED

- Recycled boxes in a variety of shapes
- Recycled paper towel and toilet paper tubes
- Tempera paint
- Paint brush
- Water
- Scissors
- Glue
- Tape
- An assortment of colored construction paper or tissue paper, cut into small square shapes
- Table covering

DIRECTIONS

1. Select a box or boxes to decorate. Add tubes to create the minarets. Secure the structure in the shape of your choice with tape or glue. If using glue, allow to dry.
2. Paint the structure a light color and allow time for drying.
3. Using the colored construction paper or tissue, cut into shapes and plan a design.
4. Glue colored paper onto your structure to create a pattern or image.

21

Ziggurats of Ancient Mesopotamia

IRAQ

Silent Music: A Story of Baghdad
James Rumford. New York, NY: Roaring Brook Press, 2008.

Ali loves playing soccer, he loves music, and he loves dancing. However, what he loves the most is calligraphy, the art of drawing letters. The flow of the letters and ink from his pen make the words dance on paper to the music in his head. Calligraphy also allows Ali to tune out the bombs of war and find the calm of peace. Photos posted by many American service personnel in Iraq inspired the stunning illustrations throughout the book.

Programming Tip

Calligraphy is an important part of Islamic culture and is used to beautify their holy book, the Qur'an. Considered the greatest calligrapher of the Arabic language, Yakut al-Musta'simi died in Baghdad in 1298. It is believed that when the Mongols attacked Baghdad in 1258, he fled to a high tower and wrote in calligraphy until the attack ceased. There are many calligraphy templates online that you can use to practice the art of writing.

ABOUT ZIGGURATS

Present day Iraq is located in what was once ancient Mesopotamia. The Sumerians dominated Mesopotamia from 3100 BC to 539 BC. This area is credited with some of the most important developments in human history, including the invention of the wheel, written cursive, mathematics, and agriculture. In the center of each Mesopotamian town, there was a ziggurat, or temple. Ancient Sumerians believed the gods lived in the sky and you needed to be close in order for them to hear your requests. The ziggurat was the tallest building in town, allowing you to be close to the gods as well as see the surrounding city.

DID YOU KNOW?

Dating back to 2100 BC, the Epic of Gilgamesh is a poem from ancient Mesopotamia. It is the earliest known surviving work of literature.

BOOKS TO DISPLAY

Joha Makes a Wish: A Middle Eastern Tale by Eric Kimmel. New York, NY: Marshall Cavendish, 2010.

The Librarian of Basra by Jeanette Winter. Orlando, FL: Harcourt, Inc, 2005.

The Golden Sandal: A Middle Eastern Cinderella Story by Rebecca Hickox. New York, NY: Holiday House, 1998.

HANDS-ON PROJECT

Ziggurats were pyramidal structures made of sun-baked bricks. They featured square, oval, or rectangular levels and were decorated with glazed bricks featuring pictures or symbols. Ziggurats had a wide base that narrowed to a flat top with built-in steps. Review the internet pictures for the Ziggurat at Ur, then practice making your own.

MATERIALS NEEDED

- Empty boxes in a variety of sizes: cereal boxes, cracker boxes, etc.
- Ruler
- Scissors
- Tape
- Glue
- Brown construction paper
- Brown paint
- Sand (optional)
- Paper plate
- Paintbrush
- Table cover

DIRECTIONS

1. Glue 3 boxes on top of one another, placing the largest at the bottom and smallest at the top.
2. Once the glue has dried, add brown paint to a paper plate, and then paint the boxes. If you have sand available, add a small amount to the paint on the plate before painting your ziggurat to add texture to the building. Allow the paint to completely dry.
3. Using brown construction paper, cut strips of paper then fold back and forth at one-inch intervals to make a staircase.
4. Using tape, attach the stairs to connect each level of the ziggurat.

22

Saint Patrick's Day

IRELAND

How to Catch a Leprechaun
Adam Wallace. Naperville, IL: Sourcebooks Jabberwocky, 2016.

Children can be quite tricky, but not as tricky as a leprechaun. In this rhyming tale, a trickster leprechaun shares all the ways children have tried to trap him. He escapes them all, leaving plenty of his own mischief behind.

Programming Tip

Lucky Charms are magically delicious, especially on St. Patrick's Day. Pass out bar graph paper, along with a variety of the magic marshmallows to each student. Have them count how many of each type of marshmallow they have, and then mark the amount on the graph. You can also offer graphing with paper images of St. Patrick's Day items, such as shamrocks, leprechauns, pots of gold, and rainbows.

ABOUT SAINT PATRICK'S DAY

Saint Patrick's Day, also known as the Feast of Saint Patrick, is a cultural and religious celebration held on March 17. It observes the death of St. Patrick, the patron saint of Ireland, and commemorates the arrival of Christianity in Ireland. The tradition of celebrating St. Patrick's Day actually started in the United States after Ireland's Great Potato Famine. In the 1840s, when immigrants arrived from Ireland in American cities, the Irish celebrated their nationality with parades and other traditions. Green is the signature color of decorations and shamrocks symbolize Irish Christian pride. The belief in leprechauns is also part of Irish lore. Leprechauns are known for their trickery, which they often use to protect their treasure.

DID YOU KNOW?

While there was never any royalty in Ireland, there are remains of over 30,000 castles all over Ireland. When the Normans arrived in Ireland, they brought the knowledge of building cut-stone fortifications. Castles were built as large fortified homes for clan chiefs and Anglo-Norman settlers.

BOOKS TO DISPLAY

Fiona's Luck by Teresa Bateman. Watertown, MA: Charlesbridge, 2007.

O'Sullivan Stew: A Tale Cooked Up in Ireland by Hudson Talbott. New York, NY: Putnam & Sons, 1999.

Jamie O'Rourke and the Big Potato: An Irish Folktale by Tomie dePaola. New York, NY: Putnam & Sons, 1992.

Tim O'Toole and the Wee Folk by Gerald McDermott. New York, NY: Viking, 1990.

HANDS-ON PROJECT

Leprechauns are fast and tricky, but if you catch one, they are required to tell you where they keep their treasure. Using a variety of household items and your imagination, create your own trap for the leprechauns.

MATERIALS NEEDED

- Paper bag, can be a grocery bag or a large lunch sack
- 1 sheet of construction paper
- 3 pipe cleaners
- 1 toilet paper roll
- 1 muffin liner
- 2 clothespins
- 1 straight straw
- 3 craft sticks
- 24 inches of yarn or twine
- Glue stick
- Crayons or colored pencils
- Assorted empty boxes such as cereal boxes, shoe boxes, tissue boxes, etc.
- Scissors
- Tape

DIRECTIONS

1. Place the empty boxes, scissors, crayons, tape, and glue sticks on a table for the students use.
2. Place the remaining loose items into the paper bag to create a mystery bag for each student to use.
3. Distribute a mystery bag of items to each student. Tell the students that they may use any box of their choice, along with the items in their bag, to create a leprechaun trap.
4. Allow students to take their trap home. As an extension activity, ask them to write a paragraph explaining whether their trap caught a leprechaun.

23

Cherry Blossom Festival

JAPAN

Wabi Sabi

Mark Reibstein. New York, NY: Little, Brown & Co., 2008.

Wabi Sabi, a cat, asks her owner and all the animals she meets the meaning of her name. While most are unable to tell her the meaning, she finally discovers that the term "wabi sabi" is more of a feeling and way of seeing the world that is central to Japanese culture. Using sparse text and haiku, *Wabi Sabi* is a story of finding beauty in the unexpected and being in harmony with all aspects of the natural world.

Programming Tip

Haiku is a short, traditional Japanese poem. The first line has five syllables, the second line has seven syllables, and the third line has five syllables. Matsuo Basho (1644–1694) is considered the greatest haiku writer and documented many of his epic journeys through haiku. Mark Reibstein features Basho's haikus in *Wabi Sabi*. After reading *Wabi Sabi*, practice writing your own nature haikus.

ABOUT THE CHERRY BLOSSOM FESTIVAL

Japan is known around the world for celebrating hanami, or cherry blossom festivals. The tradition of viewing flowers dates back to when aristocrats were inspired to write poetry after looking at the beautiful cherry blossoms. Today, people often picnic under the trees during the festivals when blossoms are at their peak. Cherry blossoms last only a week or two and serve as a symbol, reminding us that nothing last forever. Outside of Japan, one of the largest Cherry Blossom festivals is in Washington D.C., US, which hosts a National Cherry Blossom Festival that commemorates the gift of 3,000 cherry trees to the United States in 1912.

DID YOU KNOW?

Japan consists of four main islands and dozens of smaller isles. Mount Fuji, which stands at 12,388 feet, is a dormant volcano that last erupted in 1707. Japan is located within the area of the Pacific Ocean known as the Ring of Fire. Nearly 90% of the world's earthquakes take place along the Ring of Fire.

BOOKS TO DISPLAY

The Beckoning Cat: Based on a Japanese Folktale by Koko Nishizuka. New York, NY: Holiday House, 2009.

Suki's Kimono by Chieri Uegaki. New York, NY: Kids Can Press, 2005.

Three Samurai Cats by Eric Kimmel. New Nork, NY: Holiday House, 2003.

The Way We Do It in Japan by Geneva Cobb Iijima. Morton Grove, IL: Albert Whitman & Co., 2002.

Yoko's Paper Cranes by Rosemary Wells. New York, NY: Hyperion Books for Children, 2001.

HANDS-ON PROJECT

Origami is the Japanese traditional art of paper folding. After reading *Yoko's Paper Cranes,* create your own simple origami projects.

MATERIALS NEEDED

- 8-inch square piece of origami or thin paper, not construction paper
- Markers, crayons, or colored pencils

DIRECTIONS / Origami Cat

1. Hold the paper so that it is in a diamond shape, and then fold in half.
2. Fold each of the top two corners halfway down on each side.
3. Make a second fold on each side about one-half inch from the first fold.
4. Flip the point of each folded side up to make the cat ears.
5. Decorate as desired with eyes, nose, mouth, etc.

DIRECTIONS / Origami Dog

1. Hold the paper so that it is in a diamond shape, and then fold in half.
2. Fold the corners down to make floppy ears.
3. Decorate as desired with eyes, nose, mouth, etc.

Day of the Dead

MEXICO

Dia de Los Muertos

Roseanne Thong. Chicago, IL: Albert Whitman & Co., 2015.

Families throughout the town prepare to celebrate and honor their deceased loved ones on Dia de los Muertos. Rhyming text tells of families busy with their holiday preparations, from creating an altar of remembrance to putting on makeup and dressing like ghosts. Spanish words are sprinkled throughout the text. Illustrations enhance the story and incorporate many of the better-known symbols of the Day of the Dead.

ABOUT THE DAY OF THE DEAD

The Day of the Dead is a time to remember deceased loved ones. Celebrated each year from October 31 until November 2, it combines the ancient Aztec custom of remembering ancestors with All Soul's Day, a holiday that Spanish invaders brought to Mexico in the early 1500s. Altars of the departed are set up in homes so that spirits can find their way back to their relatives and are decorated with marigolds, candles, mementos, and favorite foods. "Bread of the dead" is a sweet bread baked only for this holiday and has a tiny skeleton doll inside. If the skeleton is in your piece of bread, your wish will come true. Sugar skulls come in bright colors and are eaten at the end of the celebration. On the night of November 2, families visit the cemetery where they dance, sing, share memories of their loved ones, and picnic. At the end of the celebration, families leave flowers on the graves of their loved ones.

Did You Know?

The ruins of the pre-Hispanic city of Chichen Itza are located in the Yucatan peninsula of Mexico. Built by the Mayan people, Chichen Itza was one of the largest Mayan cities during its peak from 600–900 AD and the principal ceremonial center of the Yucatan. Chichen Itza is one of the Seven Wonders of the Modern World.

PROGRAMMING TIP

There is much in the news about immigrants crossing our borders. Two recently released books celebrate those who made the risky journey to dream of a new life. For a positive look at what immigrants bring our country, share these titles with your class.

Dreamers by Yuyi Morales. New York, NY: Neal Porter Books, 2018.

> Yuyi Morales shares her story of immigration from Mexico to the United States with her infant son, leaving behind everything she knew. *Dreamers* is a celebration of the gifts migrants bring with them when they leave their homes.

La Frontera: My Journey with Papa by Deborah Mills. Cambridge, MA: Barefoot Books, 2018.

> *La Frontera* tells the story of a boy and his father on their journey from Mexico to Texas in the 1980s, including their struggles to cross the border and their success in making the United States their home. Text is in both Spanish and English.

BOOKS TO DISPLAY

Coco: Miguel and the Grand Harmony by Matt de la Pena. Los Angeles, CA: Disney Press, 2017.

Daniela's Day of the Dead by Lisa Bullard. Minneapolis, MN: Millbrook Press, 2013.

The Day of the Dead by Bob Barner. New York, NY: Holiday House, 2010.

HANDS-ON PROJECT

Skulls are one of the most recognizable symbols of the Day of the Dead. Whether sugar skulls or face paint, skulls are prominent throughout the holiday. Make your own lantern to celebrate the Day of the Dead, decorated with a brightly colored skull.

MATERIALS NEEDED

- Mason jar
- Light color glow-in-the-dark acrylic paint or glow-in-the-dark spray paint
- Paint brush
- Colored sharpie markers
- Battery-operated tea light
- Table cover

DIRECTIONS

1. Cover your work surface with a protective cover.
2. Using either acrylic paint or spray paint, apply glow in the dark paint to Mason jar and allow to dry.
3. Show pictures of decorative skulls to the class. Using sharpie markers, add details to the smooth side of a mason jar to create a skull. Include eyes, nose, a mouth, and decorative details.
4. Once the jar is completely dry, add a battery-operated tea light inside.

25

Trans-Siberian Railway

RUSSIA

The Gigantic Turnip
Aleksei Tolstoy. Brooklyn, NY: Barefoot Books, 1999.

In this traditional Russian tale, a farmer grows a turnip so big that it takes the combined efforts of him, his wife, six canaries, five geese, four hens, three cats, two pigs, one cow, and, finally, one tiny mouse to pull it from the ground. With heaving, pulling, tugging, and a "POP," the gigantic turnip comes out! As a treat for all who helped, the old man and woman make a gigantic pot of turnip stew.

ABOUT THE TRANS-SIBERIAN RAILWAY

Officially completed in 1916, the Trans-Siberian Railway crosses more than 5,000 miles. Construction began in 1891 in an attempt to connect the European part of the Russian Empire to the isolated areas in Siberia and Far East. Building took place simultaneously from both sides, working toward the center. Extreme weather, harsh landscapes, and a high financial cost made construction a tremendous undertaking. At its peak, nearly 90,000 people were involved in the construction of the railway. The Trans-Siberian Railway connects Moscow, Mongolia, and China via multiple routes. The newest line allows you to travel between Moscow and Beijing in a week.

Programming Tip

How Mama Brought the Spring by Fran Manushkin tells the delightful story of Rosy insisting she will not get out of bed until spring arrives. Rosy's mother lures her out of bed with the promise of the story of how her grandmother brought spring to Minsk, Russia. The end of the book features a recipe for blintzes that make a wonderful treat on a cold day.

DID YOU KNOW?

Established in 2009, the Russian Artic National Park is home to polar bears, narwhals, bowhead whales, walrus, seals, and one of the largest bird colonies in the Northern Hemisphere. The park, which comprises nearly 200 islands in the Arctic, also features majestic glaciers, petrified trees, hardened lava flows, and pristine landscapes. The park provides a glimpse of a habitat that is untouched by humans.

BOOKS TO DISPLAY

Babushka's Doll by Patricia Polacco. New York, NY: Simon and Schuster, 1990.

The Mitten: A Ukrainian Folktale by Jan Brett. New York, NY: G.P. Putnam's Sons, 1989.

Rechenka's Eggs by Patricia Polacco. New York, NY: Philomel Books, 1988.

HANDS-ON PROJECT

Siberia makes up 70% of Russia and is known for its long, harsh winters. Animals and humans alike look for creative ways to stay warm. Read *The Mitten* by Jan Brett, then visit her website to create your own mitten craft. http://janbrett.com/put_the_animals_in_the_mitten.htm.

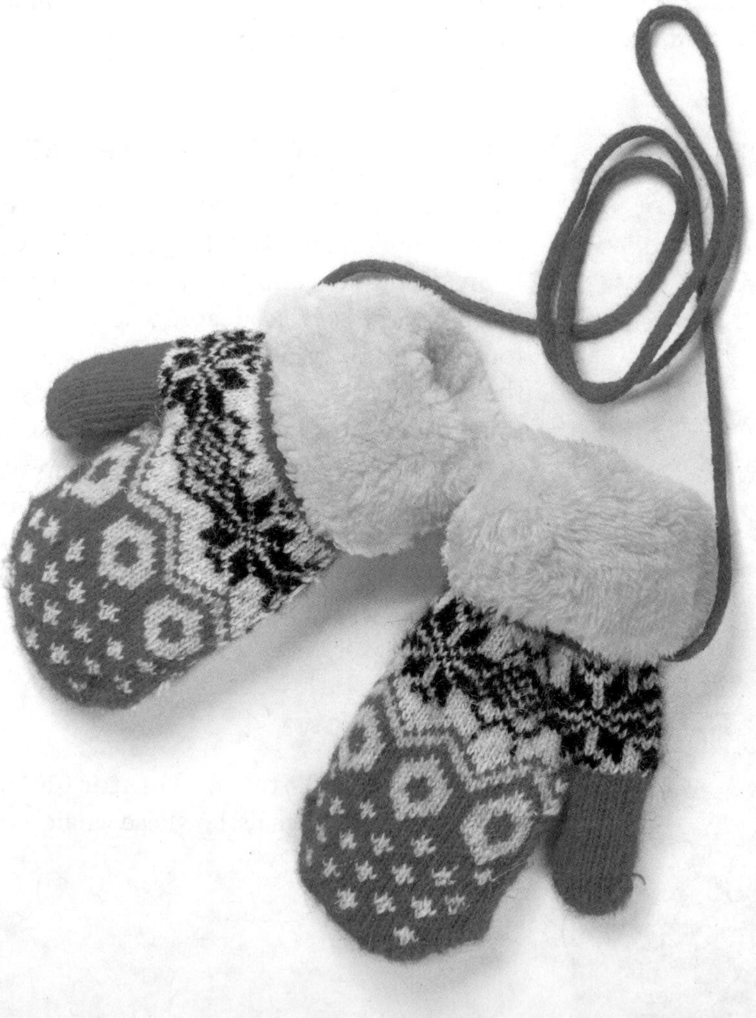

additional resources

CHAPTER 1: Iditarod Trail Sled Dog Race, Alaska, US

- Information on Alaska can be found at http://alaska.gov/.
- Information about the Iditarod National Historic Trail can be found at www.blm.gov/programs/national-conservation-lands/national-scenic-and-historic-trails/iditarod.
- Information on the life of a sled dog can be found at www.nps.gov/dena/planyourvisit/life-of-a-sled-dog.htm.
- Information on the Iditarod Trail Sled Dog Race Route can be found at http://iditarod.com/race-map/.

CHAPTER 2: Grand Canyon National Park, Arizona, US

- Information on Arizona can be found at https://az.gov/.
- Information on the Grand Canyon can be found at www.nps.gov/grca/index.htm.
- Information on the UNESCO World Heritage site for the Grand Canyon can be found at https://whc.unesco.org/en/list/75.

CHAPTER 3: Golden Gate Bridge, California, US

- Information on California can be found at www.ca.gov/.
- Information on the Golden Gate Bridge can be found at www.goldengatebridge.org/.
- Information on the 1906 San Francisco earthquake can be found at https://earthquake.usgs.gov/earthquakes/events/1906calif/18april/.

CHAPTER 4: Kennedy Space Center, Florida, US

- Information on Florida can be found at www.usa.gov/state-government/florida.
- Information about NASA, past space missions, and the future of the space program can be found at www.nasa.gov/.
- Information on the Kennedy Space Center can be found at www.kennedyspacecenter.com/.

CHAPTER 5: Lei Day Festival, Hawaii, US

- Information on Hawaii can be found at https://portal.ehawaii.gov/visitors/.
- Information on Lei making can be found at www.hawaiiflowerlei.com/makealei.aspx.
- Information on Pearl Harbor and the USS Arizona Memorial can be found at www.nps.gov/valr/index.htm.
- Information on Hawaii's National Parks can be found at www.nps.gov/state/hi/index.htm.

CHAPTER 6: Mardi Gras, New Orleans, Louisiana, US

- Information on New Orleans can be found at www.nola.gov/visitors/.
- Information on Louisiana can be found at http://louisiana.gov/.
- Information on New Orleans Events can be found at www.neworleansonline.com/calendar/.

CHAPTER 7: Chaco Culture National Historic Park, New Mexico, US

- Information on New Mexico can be found at www.newmexico.org/.
- Information on the Chaco Culture National Historic Park can be found at www.nps.gov/chcu/index.htm.
- Information on the Indian Pueblo Cultural Center can be found at www.indianpueblo.org.
- Information on the UNESCO World Heritage site for the Chaco Canyon can be found at https://whc.unesco.org/en/list/353.

CHAPTER 8: Statue of Liberty, New York, US

- Information on New York can be found at www.ny.gov/.
- Information on the Statue of Liberty can be found at www.nps.gov/stli/index.htm.
- Information about Ellis Island National Museum of Immigration can be found at www.nps.gov/elis/index.htm.

CHAPTER 9: Oregon Trail, Oregon, US

- Information on Oregon National Historic Trail can be found at www.nps.gov/oreg/index.htm.
- Information on the National Historic Oregon Trail Interpretive Center can be found at www.blm.gov/learn/interpretive-centers/national-historic-oregon-trail-interpretive-center.
- Information on the Gateway Arch Monument can be found at www.gatewayarch.com/.
- Information on Gateway Arch National Park can be found at www.nps.gov/jeff/index.htm.

CHAPTER 10: The Liberty Bell and Independence National Historic Park, Pennsylvania, US

- Information about Pennsylvania can be found at www.pa.gov/guides/exploring-pa/.
- Information about the Liberty Bell and Independence National Historic Park can be found at www.nps.gov/inde/learn/historyculture/stories-libertybell.htm.
- Information about the Benjamin Franklin Museum can be found at www.nps.gov/inde/planyourvisit/benjaminfranklinmuseum.htm.

CHAPTER 11: Mount Rushmore National Park, South Dakota, US

- Information on South Dakota can be found at https://sd.gov/.
- Information on Mount Rushmore National Memorial can be found at www.nps.gov/moru/index.htm.
- Information on Wind Cave National park can be found at www.nps.gov/wica/index.htm.

CHAPTER 12: Vaqueros and American Cowboys, Texas, US

- Information on Texas can be found at https://texas.gov/.
- Information on Vaqueros and Cowboys can be found at https://tpwd.texas.gov/education/resources/keep-texas-wild/vaqueros-and-cowboys/vaqueros.
- Information on the Galveston Hurricane of 1900 can be found at https://oceanservice.noaa.gov/news/features/sep13/galveston.html.

CHAPTER 13: The White House, Washington, D.C., US

- Information on Washington, D.C. can be found at https://dc.gov/page/visitors-resource-center.
- Information about the branches of government in the United States can be found at www.usa.gov/branches-of-government.
- Information on White House tours can be found at www.whitehouse.gov/about-the-white-house/tours-events/.
- Information about the White House can be found at www.whitehouse.gov/.

CHAPTER 14: San People, Formerly Known as the Bushmen of South Africa, Botswana, Africa

- Information on Botswana can be found at www.gov.bw/.
- Information on the Kuru Art Project can be found at www.kuruart.com/.
- Information on Chobe National Park can be found at www.chobenationalpark.com/.

CHAPTER 15: Aborigines Indigenous People, Australia

- Information on Australia can be found at www.australia.gov.au/.
- Information on Kakadu National Park, Aboriginal rock art, and the people's Aboriginal timeline can be found at https://parksaustralia.gov.au/kakadu/pub/gunbim.pdf.
- Information on the UNESCO Great Barrier Reef can be found at https://whc.unesco.org/en/list/154.

CHAPTER 16: Amazon Rainforest, Brazil

- Information on Brazil can be found at www.brasil.gov.br/.
- A short video highlighting 25 amazing Amazon Rainforest facts can be found at www.youtube.com/watch?v=DgU7gsBOhUI.

CHAPTER 17: Moon Festival, China

- China can be found at www.gov.cn/english/.
- Information on the UNESCO Great Wall of China site can be found at https://whc.unesco.org/en/list/438.

CHAPTER 18: Son Cubano Music, Cuba

- Information on Cuba can be found at www.minrex.gob.cu/en.
- A sample of Son music can be found at https://worldmusiccentral.org/tag/son-cubano/.
- National Geographic and UNESCO provide a short introductory video of Cuba at https://video.nationalgeographic.com/video/travel-source/unesco-world-heritage-sites/180912-cuba-old-havana-unesco-travel.

CHAPTER 19: Eiffel Tower, France

- Information on France can be found at www.gouvernement.fr/en/news.
- Information on the Eiffel Tower can be found at www.toureiffel.paris/en.
- Information on the Louvre can be found at www.louvre.fr/en.

CHAPTER 20: Holi Festival, India

- Information about India can be found at www.india.gov.in/.
- Information on the Holi Festival can be found at www.holifestival.org/festival-of-colours.html.
- Information on the UNESCO Taj Mahal site can be found at https://whc.unesco.org/en/list/252.

CHAPTER 21: Ziggurats of Ancient Mesopotamia, Iraq

- Information on Iraq can be found at https://gds.gov.iq/.
- Information on the Ziggurat at Ur can be found at www.khanacademy.org/humanities/ancient-art-civilizations/ancient-near-east1/sumerian/a/ziggurat-of-ur.

CHAPTER 22: Saint Patrick's Day, Ireland

- Information on Ireland can be found at www.gov.ie/en/.
- Information on some of Ireland's castles, including a short video, can be found at www.lonelyplanet.com/ireland/travel-tips-and-articles/ten-must-see-castles-in-ireland/40625c8c-8a11-5710-a052-1479d276a46a.
- Information of UNESCO's Intangible Cultural Heritage designation of Ireland's Uilleann piping can be found at https://ich.unesco.org/en/RL/uilleann-piping-01264.

CHAPTER 23: Cherry Blossom Festival, Japan

- Information on Japan can be found at www.japan.go.jp/.
- Information on haiku can be found at www.poetryfoundation.org/learn/glossary-terms/haiku-or-hokku.

CHAPTER 24: Day of the Dead, Mexico

- Information on Mexico can be found at www.gob.mx/presidencia/en.
- Information on the UNESCO Intangible Cultural Heritage of Humanity designation for Day of the Dead can be found at https://ich.unesco.org/en/RL/indigenous-festivity-dedicated-to-the-dead-00054.
- Information on the UNESCO Chichen Itza World Heritage Site can be found at https://whc.unesco.org/en/list/483.

CHAPTER 25: Trans-Siberian Railway, Russia

- Information on Russia can be found at http://government.ru/en/.
- National Geographic provides a short video of the Russian Arctic National Park at https://video.nationalgeographic.com/video/0000014d-df6d-d57d-a7ff-ffefa6c40000.
- Information on the Trans-Siberian Express can be found at www.thetranssiberianexpress.com/history.html.